WEIRD

Because normal isn't working.

Also by Craig Groeschel

Weird: Because Normal Isn't Working

The Christian Atheist: Believing in God but Living as If He Doesn't Exist

It: How Churches and Leaders Can Get It and Keep It

What Is God Really Like? (general editor)

Chazown: A Different Way to See Your Life

Going All the Way: Preparing for a Marriage That Goes the Distance

Confessions of a Pastor: Adventures in Dropping the Pose

PARTICIPANT'S GUIDE
SIX SESSIONS

WEIRD

Because normal isn't working.

CRAIG
GROESCHEL

WITH CHRISTINE M. ANDERSON

ZONDERVAN.com/
AUTHORTRACKER
follow your favorite authors

We want to hear from you. Please send your comments about this book to us in care of zreview@zondervan.com. Thank you.

ZONDERVAN

Weird Participant's Guide
Copyright © 2011 by Craig Groeschel

Requests for information should be addressed to:
Zondervan, *Grand Rapids, Michigan 49530*

ISBN 978-0-310-89498-8

Published in association with Winters, King & Associates, Inc.

Cover design: Design Works Group / Tim Green
Interior design: Ben Fetterley & Matthew Van Zomeren

Printed in the United States of America

11 12 13 14 15 16 17 /DCI/ 25 24 23 22 21 20 19 18 17 16 15 14 13 12 11 10 9 8 7 6 5 4 3 2 1

CONTENTS

HOW TO USE THIS GUIDE

Group Size

The *Weird* video curriculum is designed to be experienced in a group setting such as a Bible study, Sunday school class, or any small group gathering. To ensure everyone has enough time to participate in discussions, it is recommended that large groups break up into smaller groups of four to six people each.

Materials Needed

Each participant should have his or her own Participant's Guide, which includes video outline notes, directions for activities, and discussion questions, as well as a reading plan and personal studies to deepen learning between sessions. Although the course can be fully experienced with just the video and Participant's Guide, participants are also encouraged to have a copy of the *Weird* book. Reading the book alongside the video curriculum provides even deeper insights that make the journey richer and more meaningful.

Timing

The time notations — for example (17 minutes) — indicate the *actual* time of video segments and the *suggested* time for each activity or discussion. For example:

Individual Activity **What I Want to Remember** (2 Minutes)

Adhering to the suggested times will enable you to complete each session in one hour. If you have additional time, you may wish to allow more time for discussion and activities.

Facilitation

Each group should appoint a facilitator who is responsible for starting the video and for keeping track of time during discussions and activities. Facilitators may also read questions aloud and monitor discussions, prompting participants to respond and assuring that everyone has the opportunity to participate.

Between-Sessions Personal Study

Maximize the impact of the course with additional study between group sessions. Setting aside about an hour for personal study will enable you to complete the book and between-session studies by the end of the course. For each session, you may wish to complete the personal study all in one sitting or to spread it out over a few days.

THE GOD KIND OF WEIRD

The most spiritually dangerous things in me are the habits of thought, feeling, and action that I regard as "normal," because "everyone is like that" and "it's only human."

DALLAS WILLARD, *THE DIVINE CONSPIRACY*

Video: The God Kind of Weird (17 Minutes)

Play the video segment for session 1. As you watch, use the outline (pages 10 – 11) to follow along or to take notes on anything that stands out to you.

Notes

The problem with being normal today is that normal will get you sucked into all sorts of things that can be really hurtful to you.

Examples of how weird Jesus was (Luke 6:27 – 30):

- Love your enemies, do good to those who hate you.
- Bless those who curse you, pray for those who mistreat you.
- If someone slaps you on one cheek, turn to them the other also.
- If someone takes your coat, do not withhold your shirt from them.
- Give to everyone who asks you, and if anyone takes what belongs to you, do not demand it back.

Jesus didn't do anything like normal people did.

"Enter through the narrow gate. For wide is the gate and broad is the road that leads to destruction, and many enter through it. But small is the gate and narrow the road that leads to life, and only a few find it" (Matthew 7:13 – 14).

Normal may not be good when it comes to God.

"For it is by grace you have been saved, through faith — and this is not from yourselves, it is the gift of God — not by works, so that no one can boast" (Ephesians 2:8 – 9).

Normal is broken. Normal doesn't work.

There is a God kind of weird. It's about:

- Being different from the values of this world.
- Living for the things that will outlast this temporary world.
- Laying down your life to glorify the God of the universe.

Think about what is considered normal today:

- *Time*: overwhelmed, burdened, stressed out
- *Money*: broke, worry, debt
- *Sex*: sexual sin, promiscuity, affairs
- *Marriage*: bitterness, lack of intimacy, divorce
- *Spirituality*: lukewarm Christianity
- Normal is living for ourselves and not living for something greater.

If we are normal like everybody else, then we are not following Jesus.

When you follow Jesus, you will be called weird.

Group Discussion: The God Kind of Weird (41 Minutes)

Take a few minutes to talk about what you just watched.

1. What part of the teaching had the most impact on you?

2. Generally speaking, how do you determine what makes something normal and what makes something weird? If you can think of an example from your own experience, briefly share it.

Normal Is Broken

3. To be normal is to conform to common standards and customs. It usually means that something is ordinary, average, typical, or routine. Among people you know — family and friends — how would you describe normal attitudes and behaviors in these areas:

   • Pace of life

   • Personal finances

   • Relationships

   • Marriage/dating/sexuality

   • Spiritual life

4. In what ways, if any, does your faith community reinforce or challenge these normal attitudes and behaviors? Note any specific examples you can think of.

> Having faith often means doing what others see as crazy. Something is wrong when our lives make sense to unbelievers.
>
> Francis Chan,
> *Crazy Love*

5. How do you respond to the idea that if we are normal — like everyone else — we aren't following Jesus?

Jesus Was Weird

6. Among the weirdest things Jesus taught are countercultural ideas about how we are to treat others — both our enemies and our friends — and what our behavior toward others reveals about us. Here is what he had to say about enemies:

> But to you who are listening I say: Love your enemies, do good to those who hate you, bless those who curse you, pray for those who mistreat you. If someone slaps you on one cheek, turn to them the other also. If someone takes your coat, do not withhold your shirt from them. Give to everyone who asks you, and if anyone takes what belongs to you, do not demand it back. Do to others as you would have them do to you (Luke 6:27 – 31).

- In this passage, enemies are those who hate, curse, mistreat, slap, and steal from us. How would you describe a normal response to this kind of behavior?

- Have you, or has someone you know, responded to mistreatment in the way Jesus describes — with love, blessings, prayer, generosity, forgiveness? Briefly describe the situation and what happened as a result.

7. After addressing enemies, Jesus also challenges any notions about virtue based on how we treat our friends:

> If you love those who love you, what credit is that to you? Even sinners love those who love them. And if you do good to those who are good to you, what credit is that to you? Even sinners do that. And if you lend to those from whom you expect repayment, what credit is that to you? Even sinners lend to sinners, expecting to be repaid in full (Luke 6:32 – 34).

- What do you think Jesus means by "credit"?

- Jesus challenges his followers to be different from "sinners." Based on these verses, how would you describe what it means to be different?

Weird God's Way

8. Jesus makes it clear that the standard we are to follow is based not on the normal behavior of others — enemies or friends — but on the weird way God treats us.

> I started to think that maybe I should beware of things that are cool and normal, because Jesus didn't seem to be either of those.... You don't get crucified for being cool; you get crucified for living radically different from the norms of all that is cool in the world.
>
> Shane Claiborne,
> *The Irresistible Revolution*

But love your enemies, do good to them, and lend to them without expecting to get anything back. Then your reward will be great, and you will be children of the Most High, because he is kind to the ungrateful and wicked. Be merciful, just as your Father is merciful (Luke 6:35 – 36).

- When you think of those who might be enemies in your life right now, what makes it difficult for you to be weird God's way — to treat your enemies with love, goodness, generosity, kindness, and mercy?

- Even if your efforts to love those who are hard to love seem to have no impact on them, how do you imagine those efforts might impact you?

Individual Activity: What I Want to Remember (2 Minutes)

Complete this activity on your own.

1. Briefly review the video outline and any notes you took.

2. In the space below, write down the most significant thing you gained in this session — from the teaching, activities, or discussions.

   What I want to remember from this session ...

Closing Prayer

Close your time together with prayer.

Between-Sessions Personal Study

● READ AND REFLECT

Read the introduction to *Weird*. Use the space below to note any insights or questions you want to bring to the next group session.

● DANGEROUSLY NORMAL

"Normal" is what we want to hear the doctor say when we've had a medical test, but it's probably not the assessment we want anyone to make of our spiritual health. When it comes to our relationship with God, normal may not be good; in fact, it might be dangerous.

> The problem with being normal is that normal today will get you sucked into all sorts of things that can actually be really hurtful to you.... What is normal today doesn't make people happy or fulfilled.
>
> *Weird* video

1. Use the following chart to briefly assess what constitutes "normal" in your life right now. For each area of life, consider attitudes as well as behaviors. How do you typically think, feel, and act in this area?

AREA OF LIFE	WHAT'S NORMAL FOR ME RIGHT NOW
Pace of Life *flexibility, scheduling, levels of fatigue or rest*	

Personal Finances *earning, giving, saving, spending, debt*	
Relationships *family members, friends, colleagues, neighbors*	
Marriage/Dating/ Sexuality *intimacy, connection, affirmation, communication, commitment, integrity*	
Spiritual Life *desire for God, practice of spiritual disciplines (prayer, solitude, journaling, etc.), growth in love of God and others*	
Other	

Based on your chart, how would you assess your normal life right now? Circle the number below that best describes your response.

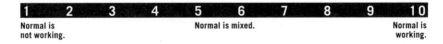

1	2	3	4	5	6	7	8	9	10

Normal is
not working.   Normal is mixed.   Normal is
                                                                                                    working.

In what area of life would you say normal is most broken for you?

2. Author and pastor Dallas Willard writes, "The most spiritually dangerous things in me are the habits of thought, feeling, and action that I regard as 'normal,' because 'everyone is like that' and 'it's only human.'" In what ways, if any, have similar thoughts influenced you in the area of life that is most broken for you?

Example

The area of my life that is most broken: personal finances

My habits of thought ... I can't afford to give financially. Money is tight for everyone right now.

My habits of feeling ... I've had a hard week and I need a treat. Buying that gadget will make me feel better. Everyone deserves a little reward now and then.

My habits of action ... I'll charge it now and figure out how to pay for it later. Everyone carries some credit card debt.

The area of my life that is most broken: _____

My habits of thought ...

My habits of feeling ...

My habits of action ...

How might these habits of thought, feeling, and action be spiritually dangerous for you?

If you choose not to coast along the world's wide-open road but rather to blaze a narrow trail with Jesus as your guide, then you'll never settle for normal again. You'll want only one thing. The God kind of weird.

Weird, page 20

3. The broad route is often the normal route, the one most people follow. But Jesus taught that the broad route won't lead us to the life he wants us to have:

> Enter through the narrow gate. For wide is the gate and broad is the road that leads to destruction, and many enter through it. But small is the gate and narrow the road that leads to life, and only a few find it (Matthew 7:13 – 14).

- The metaphor of broad and narrow gates implies that there are some things that won't fit through a narrow gate. What might you have to let go of in order to pass through the small gate or walk the narrow road that leads to life?

- Read the Matthew passage again from *The Message*:

> Don't look for shortcuts to God. The market is flooded with surefire, easygoing formulas for a successful life that can be practiced in your spare time. Don't fall for that stuff, even though crowds of people do. The way to life — to God! — is vigorous and requires total attention (Matthew 7:13 – 14 MSG).

The passage contrasts practicing faith in our spare time with giving God our total attention. How do you recognize these contrasts in your own life? Answer this question by completing the two sentences at the top of page 20.

I know I'm taking shortcuts or practicing faith in my spare time when ...

I know I am devoting total attention to my faith when ...

> If you take the Bible seriously, I trust you won't deny that the way normal people live today is miles away from what God intended. Separating ourselves from what the world considers normal is not just a matter of obedience. God invites us to dance to a different tune, because he knows what's truly going to satisfy and fulfill us.
>
> *Weird*, page 20

4. In what ways do you think God might be inviting you to dance to a different tune?

What concerns, if any, does God's invitation raise?

What hopes does God's invitation stir up in you?

The kind of weird God invites us to be isn't a bad kind of weird or a weird merely for the sake of being weird. It's about being different for a purpose — becoming more like Christ and discovering the weird blessings of living God's way.

IT'S TIME TO
BE WEIRD

To allow oneself to be carried away by a multitude of conflicting concerns, to surrender to too many demands, to commit oneself to too many projects, to want to help everyone in everything, is to succumb to the violence of our times.

THOMAS MERTON, *CONJECTURES OF A GUILTY BYSTANDER*

Group Discussion: Checking In (5 Minutes)

Welcome to session 2 of *Weird*. A key part of getting to know God better is sharing your journey with others. Before watching the video, briefly check in with each other about your experiences since the last session. For example:

- What insights did you discover in the personal study or in the introduction you read from the *Weird* book?
- How did the last session impact your daily life or your relationship with God?
- What questions would you like to ask the other members of your group?

Video: It's Time to Be Weird (17 Minutes)

Play the video segment for session 2. As you watch, use the outline (pages 22–24) to follow along or to take notes on anything that stands out to you.

Notes

Normal is being overwhelmed.

Instead of spending time on the important, we often spend time on the urgent.

Mary and Martha (Luke 10:38 – 42)

A busy lifestyle doesn't mean that we're important; it simply means we're busy.

"Do not conform to the pattern of this world, but be transformed by the renewing of your mind. Then you will be able to test and approve what God's will is — his good, pleasing and perfect will" (Romans 12:2).

To be truly weird in the best sort of way, we have to have the courage to say no to what many people say yes to.

Why do we have good intentions when it comes to our time investment but rarely follow through? Because, ultimately, we don't trust God. We have a lack of faith.

We are trying to find meaning in what we do rather than in who we are.

You have to learn to say no to some good things in order to say yes to the best things.

You have enough time for what you choose to have time for. You are in control of your time.

"Come to me, all you who are weary and burdened, and I will give you rest. Take my yoke upon you and learn from me, for I am gentle and humble in heart, and you will find rest for your souls" (Matthew 11:28 – 29).

"Be still, and know that I am God" (Psalm 46:10).

Group Discussion: It's Time to Be Weird (5 Minutes)

Take a few minutes to talk about what you just watched.

1. What part of the teaching had the most impact on you?

2. How do you respond to the idea that our inability to slow down and be more intentional with our time demonstrates a lack of trust in God?

> Hurry is not just a disordered schedule. Hurry is a disordered heart.
>
> John Ortberg, *The Life You've Always Wanted*

Group Activity: Time Out (5 Minutes)

1. Appoint one person to be a timekeeper or set a timer on your watch or phone for 5 minutes.

2. Set aside your study materials so your hands and lap are empty and then settle into a comfortable position.

3. Start the timer and spend 5 minutes together in silence. As you begin, you may wish to close your eyes, inhale deeply, and exhale slowly. Silently ask God to help you rest in him.

4. When 5 minutes have passed, the timekeeper closes your time of silence by saying, "Amen."

Group Discussion (26 Minutes)

Time Out

1. How did you experience the 5 minutes? Did it seem like it would never end, or did it go by much too quickly for you?

2. What were you aware of in the silence? For example, did a thousand thoughts rush through your mind? Did you notice any particular emotions? Did you feel awkward or completely at rest?

3. Do you feel resistant to this kind of silent resting in God, or is it something you feel drawn to? Why?

Choosing Time

4. On the video, Craig uses the story of Mary and Martha to illustrate that we have a choice about how we spend our time. As you read the story aloud, listen for insights about the choices the two women make between what's urgent and what's important.

> As Jesus and his disciples were on their way, he came to a village where a woman named Martha opened her home to him. She had a sister called Mary, who sat at the Lord's feet listening to what he said. But Martha was distracted by all the preparations that had to be made. She came to him and asked, "Lord, don't you care that my sister has left me to do the work by myself? Tell her to help me!"
>
> "Martha, Martha," the Lord answered, "you are worried and upset about many things, but few things are needed — or indeed only one. Mary has chosen what is better, and it will not be taken away from her" (Luke 10:38 – 42).

- Using Martha as an example, how would you describe a life characterized by spending time on what's urgent?

- Using Mary as an example, how would you describe a life characterized by spending time on what's important?

- Do you think Martha felt she had a choice about how to spend her time? Why or why not?

> There are limits to my capacities relationally, emotionally, mentally and spiritually. I am not God. God is the One who can be all things to all people. God is the One who can be two places at once. God is the One who never sleeps. I am not.
>
> Ruth Haley Barton, *Sacred Rhythms*

- What makes it difficult for you to choose to spend time on what's important rather than what's urgent? If possible, share an example from your own experience to illustrate your response.

5. It takes courage to say no to what most people say yes to. What personal commitment would you like to say no to if you had the courage to do so? What makes this commitment especially hard to step away from?

Time to Be Still

6. Listed below are five versions of Psalm 46:10. Go around the group and have a different person read each verse aloud. As the verses are read, underline any words or phrases that stand out to you. You may wish to read through the list twice to give everyone time to listen and respond.

> Be still, and know that I am God! (NLT)
> Cease striving and know that I am God. (NASB)
> Step out of the traffic! Take a long, loving look at me, your High God. (MSG)
> Calm down, and learn that I am God! (CEV)
> Let be and be still, and know (recognize and understand) that I am God. (AMP)

- Which version of the verse stands out most to you? Why?

- What, if anything, keeps you from making the choice to be still?

- In what area of your life do you most need to know that God is God?

Individual Activity: What I Want to Remember (2 Minutes)

Complete this activity on your own.

1. Briefly review the video outline and any notes you took.

2. In the space below, write down the most significant thing you gained in this session — from the teaching, activities, or discussions.

   What I want to remember from this session ...

Closing Prayer

Close your time together with prayer.

Between-Sessions Personal Study

● READ AND REFLECT

Read chapters 1, 2, and 3 of *Weird*. Use the space below to note any insights or questions you want to bring to the next group session.

● GOOD TIME OR BEST TIME?

Most of the normal activities that fill up our schedules aren't bad things; in fact, they are often good things. The challenge comes when too many good things become the enemy of the best things — the kind of life God wants us to have and the kind of people he wants us to become.

> The barrier to a meaningful life for many of us is not that we're not committed enough; it's that we're overly committed, doing way too much.... We have to be willing to say no — to be very different from this world — in order to please God with our time.
>
> *Weird* video

1. Use the five questions that follow to briefly assess your current pace of life.

   a. How would you describe your schedule during a typical week? Check the box next to the phrase that best describes your response.

   ☐ *Time surplus.* I am unscheduled. I have virtually no commitments.

   ☐ *Time available.* I am lightly scheduled. I have only a few commitments and a lot of discretionary time.

   ☐ *Time balanced.* I am moderately scheduled. I have a good mix of commitments and discretionary time.

   ☐ *Time limited.* I am heavily scheduled. I have several commitments and little discretionary time.

   ☐ *Time deficit.* I am overscheduled. I have too many commitments and virtually no discretionary time.

b. How much control do you feel you have over your schedule right now? Place an X on the continuum to indicate your response.

●————————————————————●

I have no control
over my schedule.

I have complete
control over my schedule.

c. "My current schedule enables me to bring my best self to my tasks, to my relationships, and to God." To what degree is this statement true of you?

☐ Not at all true of me.
☐ Somewhat true of me.
☐ Moderately true of me.
☐ Mostly true of me.
☐ Completely true of me.

d. "I have adequate time and energy to care for myself physically — to sleep, eat healthy, and exercise." To what degree is this statement true of you?

☐ Not at all true of me.
☐ Somewhat true of me.
☐ Moderately true of me.
☐ Mostly true of me.
☐ Completely true of me.

e. "I believe that God is just as pleased with me when I'm resting and still as he is when I'm active and busy." To what degree is this statement true of you?

☐ Not at all true of me.
☐ Somewhat true of me.
☐ Moderately true of me.
☐ Mostly true of me.
☐ Completely true of me.

Based on your responses to the five questions, how would you describe the impact your pace of life has on you — physically, emotionally, relationally, spiritually?

Physically ...

Emotionally ...

Relationally ...

Spiritually ...

[Jesus] was busy but never hurried. He was productive but never overwhelmed. He accomplished everything God wanted him to do and still spent long, refreshing days in fellowship alone with his Father. Knowing when and how to rest is knowing when and how to acknowledge your limitations and your dependence on God.

Weird, pages 54–55

2. Jesus was often in high demand, but he never allowed those demands to control him. In fact, he typically took time out from his work to rest and pray.

> The apostles returned to Jesus from their ministry tour and told him all they had done and taught. Then Jesus said, "Let's go off by ourselves to a quiet place and rest awhile." He said this because there were so many people coming and going that Jesus and his apostles didn't even have time to eat. So they left by boat for a quiet place, where they could be alone (Mark 6:30 – 32 NLT).

> News about Jesus kept spreading. Large crowds came to listen to him teach and to be healed of their diseases. But Jesus would often go to some place where he could be alone and pray (Luke 5:15 – 16 CEV).

- Based on these passages, what do you notice about when Jesus chose to rest?

- How did Jesus choose to rest? What conditions were essential?

- How did Jesus' decisions related to rest acknowledge his human limitations and dependence on God?

- Are you able to choose times of intentional rest in the midst of your schedule, or do you take only the rest you can get when your schedule allows?

- Overall, would you say your decisions about when and how to rest acknowledge or defy your human limitations? Affirm or deny your dependence on God?

Often instead of asking, "Is this right or wrong?" or "Will I enjoy this or not?" we need to ask, "Is this wise in light of my desire to stay grounded in what matters most to me and to God?"
Weird, page 44

3. Think of a commitment you made that you later regretted making. It might be an ongoing commitment for something like volunteer work, or perhaps it was just a onetime event. Imagine that this is a commitment you haven't yet made. Briefly describe the commitment in the space below and then use the three questions on the chart to evaluate the commitment.

QUESTION	YES OR NO? WHY?
1. Is this right or wrong?	
2. Will I enjoy this?	
3. Is this wise in light of my desire to stay grounded in what matters most to me and God?	

- Would your responses to each of the questions on the chart lead you to make different decisions (i.e., one decision in response to question 1 and a different decision in response to question 2, etc.), or would your responses to all three questions lead you to the same decision? Why?

- When you think about your existing commitments, which (if any) wouldn't pass question 3 on the chart: *Is this wise in light of my desire to stay grounded in what matters most to me and God?* Briefly list these commitments below.

- What prevents you from stepping down from these commitments?

Just as your body needs sleep, your soul needs time to rest in God.

Weird, page 59

4. The psalmist sees rest as a sign of God's goodness and his love.

> Return to your rest, my soul, for the LORD has been good to you (Psalm 116:7).

> Unless the LORD builds a house, the work of the builders is wasted. Unless the LORD protects a city, guarding it with sentries will do no good. It is useless for you to work so hard from early morning until late at night, anxiously working for food to eat; for God gives rest to his loved ones (Psalm 127:1 – 2 NLT).

- The Hebrew word used for "rest" in Psalm 116 is *mānôaḥ* (mah-noʹ-akh), which means a resting place. The root word conveys the image of a roost or a place to land.[1] Like birds, souls need a place to roost and rest in safety. Which image best describes your soul right now — a bird in constant flight with no place to land or a bird safely resting on a roost? Why?

The passage from Psalm 127 repeatedly stresses the futility of self-reliance — anything not undertaken in partnership with God is "wasted," "no good," and "useless." In contrast to working anxiously to provide for ourselves, God invites us to be his loved ones, to rely on his provision, and to demonstrate our trust by accepting his gift of rest.

- How does self-reliance evidence itself in the choices you make about things like how to spend your time, how hard you work, or how anxious you feel about your security?

---

1. John N. Oswalt, *New International Dictionary of Old Testament Theology and Exegesis*, vol. 3, Willem A. Van Gemeren, gen. ed. (Grand Rapids: Zondervan, 1997), 56 – 57.

- Do you tend to think of God more as someone who gives you a list of things to do or as someone who invites you to rest? How do the Psalms passages impact your view of God and how God feels about you?

- What, if anything, makes it difficult for you to accept God's gift of rest?

You don't have to buy into the normal routines of always working faster, harder, longer; clutching busyness and activity to earn acceptance or bolster a facade of significance. When it comes to time, it is wise to be weird — to say no to the good to make room for the best. To pause long enough to receive the embrace of a Savior whose gentle invitation to tired souls is this: "Come to me, all you who are weary and burdened, and I will give you rest" (Matthew 11:28).

WEIRD THAT MONEY CAN'T BUY

There are three conversions necessary: the conversion of the heart, mind, and the purse.

MARTIN LUTHER

Group Discussion: Checking In (5 Minutes)

Welcome to session 3 of *Weird*. A key part of getting to know God better is sharing your journey with others. Before watching the video, briefly check in with each other about your experiences since the last session. For example:

- What insights did you discover in the personal study or in the chapters you read from the *Weird* book?
- How did the last session impact your daily life or your relationship with God?
- What questions would you like to ask the other members of your group?

Video: Weird That Money Can't Buy (18 Minutes)

Play the video segment for session 3. As you watch, use the outline (pages 38–39) to follow along or to take notes on anything that stands out to you.

Notes

Normal is ...

- living paycheck to paycheck
- always worrying about money
- financial tension
- fear
- fighting about money
- wanting to give but not having the financial margin to do so

Financial margin: the difference between what you have and what you need

Weird is God calling you to do something with money and not having to worry, "Where am I going to get the money?"

"The wise store up choice food and olive oil, but a foolish man devours all he has" (Proverbs 21:20).

The culture's definition of happiness: "more than I currently have"

People today have a spiritual problem because they're trying to find meaning in the things of this world.

If you don't have margin, you need to earn more or spend less.

One of the greatest responsibilities we have as Christians is to wisely manage the resources God puts in our care.

Two things happen when you put God first in your finances:

    1. You become supernaturally content (Proverbs 15:16).

    2. You end up with more of what matters (Proverbs 8:18 – 19).

"You will be made rich [enriched] in every way so that you can be generous on every occasion, and through us your generosity will result in thanksgiving to God" (2 Corinthians 9:11).

Group Discussion: Weird That Money Can't Buy (35 Minutes)

Take a few minutes to talk about what you just watched.

1. What part of the teaching had the most impact on you?

2. Generally speaking, what is your initial response to the topic of God and money? For example, discomfort, intrigue, guilt, curiosity, etc.

The Normal Challenges of Money

3. Which two or three phrases listed below best characterize the financial struggles of people you know — friends, family, colleagues, neighbors, etc.?

☐ Living paycheck to paycheck
☐ Worried about making payments
☐ Financial tension
☐ Afraid of not having enough
☐ Living on the edge of financial disaster
☐ Fighting about money
☐ Unable or unwilling to save

☐ Wanting to give but not being able to
☐ Being broke
☐ Unwilling to live within their means
☐ Incurring debt
☐ Financing lifestyle with credit cards
☐ Other:

In what ways, if any, do you relate to these same struggles?

4. Recall a purchase that initially excited you but later disappointed you. It might be something small like a pair of shoes or a piece of clothing, or perhaps something larger such as a computer, a piece of furniture, or a vacation.

- What were your expectations about what you were purchasing? For example, what benefits did you anticipate? How did you imagine having this item would make you feel?

- On the video, Craig states that culture's definition of happiness is "more than I currently have." Do you think this cultural influence was a factor in your purchase? Why or why not?

> Jesus knew ... that questions regarding money go right to the heart of each individual, and he treated the issue as a deeply spiritual matter.
>
> Jim Wallis,
> The Call to Conversion

Putting God First

5. Jesus told a parable about the rich fool, a man whose preoccupation with accumulating material wealth revealed a tragically impoverished relationship with God (Luke 12:16 – 21). Jesus then instructed his disciples not to be overly concerned about material possessions or needs:

> Don't worry about such things. These things dominate the thoughts of unbelievers all over the world, but your Father already knows your needs. Seek the Kingdom of God above all else, and he will give you everything you need. So don't be afraid, little flock. For it gives your Father great happiness to give you the Kingdom (Luke 12:29 – 32 NLT).

- What emotions does Jesus address in his teaching? In what ways might these emotions fuel a preoccupation with material needs?

- The passage uses the Greek word *epizēteō* (ep-ee-dzay-teh-o) to describe how material concerns can dominate our thoughts. *Epizēteō* means to seek after, strive for, or search for.[2] Jesus contrasts this intense seeking of material things with seeking the kingdom of God "above all else." What do you think it might mean in practical terms to "seek the kingdom of God above all else" in the following uses of money:

  Earning

  Saving

  Giving

  Spending

  Incurring debt

6. What reservations or concerns come to mind when you consider what it might mean for you to put God first — above all else — in the way you view and use money? What encouragement or hopes come to mind?

---

2. Hans Georg Link, "Seek, Find," *New International Dictionary of New Testament Theology*, vol. 3, Colin Brown, gen. ed. (Grand Rapids: Zondervan, 1978, 1986), 530.

More of What Matters

7. Here is how the apostle Paul describes what happens when we put God first:

> Yes, you will be enriched in every way so that you can always be generous. And when we take your gifts to those who need them, they will thank God (2 Corinthians 9:11 NLT).

> The concept of downgrading so that others might upgrade is biblical, beautiful ... and nearly unheard of.
>
> Francis Chan,
> *Crazy Love*

- The Greek word used for "generous" is *haplotēs* (hap-lot´-ace). It means simplicity, sincerity, and uprightness. It conveys the idea of personal wholeness, undividedness, and singleness of heart.[3] Which of these aspects of being generous do you feel most drawn to or curious about? Why?

> The discipline of sacrifice is one in which we forsake the security of meeting our needs with what is in our hands. It is total abandonment to God, a stepping into the darkened abyss in the faith and hope that God will bear us up.
>
> Dallas Willard, *The Spirit of the Disciplines*

- What meaningful experiences have you had of generosity — on either the giving or receiving end? How did your experiences impact your relationship with God?

8. On the video, Craig teaches that one of the benefits of putting God first in our finances is that we end up with more of what matters. Instead of consuming more and more, we become extravagant givers.

- Describe what you think Craig means when he uses the term "what matters."

---

3. Burkhard Gärtner, "Simplicity, Sincerity, Uprightness," *New International Dictionary of New Testament Theology*, vol. 3, Colin Brown, gen. ed. (Grand Rapids: Zondervan, 1978, 1986), 571–572.

- What would having more of what matters look like for you?

- How do you imagine having more of what matters might influence the way you view and use money?

9. If you had more financial margin, how would you enjoy expressing your generosity? What persons, organizations, or causes would you most like to support? Why?

Individual Activity: What I Want to Remember (2 Minutes)

Complete this activity on your own.

1. Briefly review the video outline and any notes you took.

2. In the space below, write down the most significant thing you gained in this session — from the teaching, activities, or discussions.

   What I want to remember from this session ...

Closing Prayer

Close your time together with prayer.

Between-Sessions Personal Study

● READ AND REFLECT

Read chapters 4, 5, and 6 of *Weird*. Use the space below to note any insights or questions you want to bring to the next group session.

● LIFESTYLES OF THE BLESSED AND GENEROUS

If you've ever been the recipient of someone else's generosity — especially if you were in a tough spot — you know the impact it can have. But it's not easy to be generous. In fact, sometimes it feels impossible. Finances always seem to be tighter than we'd like and there is just no margin, never enough extra to give the way we'd like, at least, not without making some changes. Heart changes and lifestyle changes — all of them high-yield, guaranteed investments in God's weird economy.

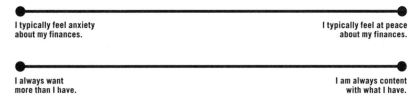

When it comes to most people's finances … normal is financial tension.

Weird video

1. Place an X on each of the continuums below and on page 46 to briefly assess your attitudes and behaviors when it comes to finances.

I typically feel anxiety
about my finances.

I typically feel at peace
about my finances.

I always want
more than I have.

I am always content
with what I have.

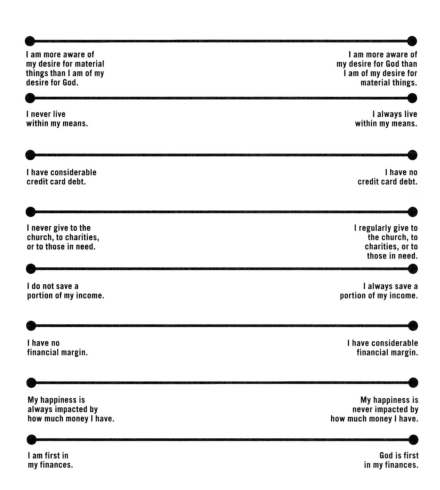

I am more aware of
my desire for material
things than I am of my
desire for God.

I am more aware of
my desire for God than
I am of my desire for
material things.

I never live
within my means.

I always live
within my means.

I have considerable
credit card debt.

I have no
credit card debt.

I never give to the
church, to charities,
or to those in need.

I regularly give to
the church, to
charities, or to
those in need.

I do not save a
portion of my income.

I always save a
portion of my income.

I have no
financial margin.

I have considerable
financial margin.

My happiness is
always impacted by
how much money I have.

My happiness is
never impacted by
how much money I have.

I am first in
my finances.

God is first
in my finances.

2. Briefly review your responses on the continuums. Imagine that everything about your financial attitudes and behaviors now will stay exactly as it is for the next ten years. What do you anticipate the cumulative impact would be on the following aspects of your life?

Finances (giving, saving, spending, debt, margin, etc.)

Emotions (contentment, happiness, peace of mind, etc.)

Spiritual growth (putting God first, growing in trust, etc.)

3. What is your initial response to your ten-year financial outlook? List four to six words or phrases. For example: concerned, encouraged, sobered, excited, overwhelmed, at peace, sad, etc.

What, if anything, would you like to be different about your ten-year financial outlook?

4. Using the analogy of planting seeds, the apostle Paul taught the church at Corinth how God not only uses but multiplies everything we give.

> Remember this — a farmer who plants only a few seeds will get a small crop. But the one who plants generously will get a generous crop. You must each decide in your heart how much to give. And don't give reluctantly or in response to pressure. "For God loves a person who gives cheerfully" (2 Corinthians 9:6 – 7 NLT).

- A farmer might take one of two views when planting seeds: every seed planted is a seed lost, or every seed planted is a harvest gained. How do you relate these two views to your own view and experience of giving?

We must go from the normal mindset about money and wealth to a radically weird view: gratitude for all we have and stewardship of its use for the good of all.

Weird, page 71

- Paul stresses a vital heart connection when it comes to giving — that *how* we give is as important as, or perhaps even more important than, *what* we give. At least three things are essential:

  1. How you decide (in your heart)
  2. What to give (an amount)
  3. How you give it (cheerfully, not reluctantly or under pressure)

Reflect on a past or recent experience of financial giving. To what degree would you say your decision was considered prayerfully and made in your heart?

How did you determine the amount you gave?

How would you characterize the way you gave (cheerfully, reluctantly, under pressure, etc.)?

How did this giving experience impact you? For example, did it make you feel generous, leave you indifferent, or strengthen your connection to God?

Weirdly enough, the more we give away, the richer we become.
Weird, page 91

5. Paul continues his teaching to the church at Corinth by describing God's generous response to our giving.

> And God will generously provide all you need. Then you will always have everything you need and plenty left over to share with others. As the Scriptures say, "They share freely and give generously to the poor. Their good deeds will be remembered forever." For God is the one who provides seed for the farmer and then bread to eat. In the same way, he will provide and increase your resources and then produce a great harvest of generosity in you. Yes, you will be enriched in every way so that you can always be generous. And when we take your gifts to those who need them, they will thank God (2 Corinthians 9:8 – 11 NLT).

- An economy is a system that manages the resources, finances, income, and expenditures of a community. Based on this passage, how would you describe God's economy?

- Paul affirms that God owns the whole supply line that stretches from seed to harvest to bread on the table. And he's generous! He shares everything he owns with us. How does the truth that God owns everything affirm or challenge the way you view and use money?

- According to the passage, how would you describe the intended impact of God's generosity on you, and of your generosity on God and others?

- If you were able to arrange your life so you could give the way the passage describes, how do you imagine it might impact your ten-year financial outlook (question 2, pages 46–47)?

Finances (giving, saving, spending, debt, margin, etc.)

Emotions (contentment, happiness, peace of mind, etc.)

Spiritual growth (putting God first, growing in trust, etc.)

> We find our lives when we give them away. As long as we live in pursuit of more stuff ... or rely on status symbols to define us ... we will never live in true abundance.
>
> *Weird*, page 71

6. Committing ourselves to God's economy is part of what it means to put God first, to seek his kingdom above all else. Then we are freed up to entrust ourselves fully into God's care.

> What I'm trying to do here is to get you to relax, to not be so preoccupied with *getting*, so you can respond to God's *giving*. People who don't know God and the way he works fuss over these things, but you know both God and how he works. Steep your life in God-reality, God-initiative, God-provisions. Don't worry about missing out. You'll find all your everyday human concerns will be met (Matthew 6:30 – 33 MSG).

- What are you worried about missing out on if you begin to focus more on giving?

- What might you enjoy doing as a response to God's giving?

Giving isn't just something we *do*. Because we are made in the image of God, generosity is part of who we *are*. When we commit to giving consistently, we grow closer to him. We pull all our resources out of the Me economy and sink everything we have — heart, soul, and finances — into God's economy.

Welcome to the lifestyle of the blessed and generous.

PLEASING GOD IS WEIRD

The Christian who cares only for God's approval lives free of the tyranny of conformist pressures, relaxed under the steady direction of the God who loves us and gives himself for us. Those who try to please the world by their good behavior very quickly find themselves under the unkind surveillance of a thousand critics.

EUGENE H. PETERSON, *A YEAR WITH JESUS*

Group Discussion: Checking In (5 Minutes)

Welcome to session 4 of *Weird*. A key part of getting to know God better is sharing your journey with others. Before watching the video, briefly check in with each other about your experiences since the last session. For example:

- What insights did you discover in the personal study or in the chapters you read from the *Weird* book?
- How did the last session impact your daily life or your relationship with God?
- What questions would you like to ask the other members of your group?

Video: Pleasing God Is Weird (17 Minutes)

Play the video segment for session 4. As you watch, use the outline (pages 52–54) to follow along or to take notes on anything that stands out to you.

Notes

Becoming obsessed with what people think about you is the quickest way to forget what God thinks about you.

It's normal to want to please people. It's weird to make God your highest priority.

A great thing to remember: I can't please everyone, but I can please God.

"Am I now trying to win the approval of human beings, or of God? Or am I trying to please people? If I were still trying to please people, I would not be a servant of Christ" (Galatians 1:10).

Four characteristics of people pleasers:

1. People pleasers tend to take criticism personally.
2. People pleasers feel an extraordinary fear of rejection.
3. People pleasers find it hard to express their true feelings.
4. People pleasers have a hard time saying no.

people pleasing =
- a spiritual
problem

People pleasing is a form of idolatry.

"But because of the Pharisees they would not confess their faith for fear they would be put out of the synagogue; for they loved praise from men more than praise from God" (John 12:42 – 43).

"Fear of man will prove to be a snare, but whoever trusts in the LORD is kept safe" (Proverbs 29:25).

Moqesh (mo-keshe´), the Hebrew word for "snare," means a noose for catching animals or a hook in the nose.

The fear of God is the best antidote for the fear of people. If people are too big in your life, it's because your God is too small.

"Fear the LORD, you his godly people, for those who fear him will have all they need" (Psalm 34:9 NLT).

The bigger your God is, the smaller your fears will become of the opinions of people.

"We are not trying to please men but God, who tests our hearts.... We were not looking for praise from men, not from you or anyone else" (1 Thessalonians 2:4, 6).

Group Discussion: Pleasing God Is Weird (36 Minutes)

Take a few minutes to talk about what you just watched.

1. What part of the teaching had the most impact on you?

2. In general, would you say that Christians tend to engage in people pleasing behaviors more than, less than, or at the same levels as non-Christians? Explain your response.

Characteristics of People Pleasers

3. On the video, Craig lists four characteristics of people pleasers:

   - People pleasers tend to take criticism personally.
   - People pleasers feel an extraordinary fear of rejection.
   - People pleasers find it hard to express their true feelings.
   - People pleasers have a hard time saying no.

   Which of the four characteristics do you relate to most? Why? If possible, illustrate your response with an example from your own experience.

4. When people engage in what is sometimes called "impression management," they try to influence how other people perceive them, often by highlighting their most attractive features and hiding anything unattractive.

> I just want everyone around me to be happy. Is that wrong?
>
> **Twitter post**

- How would you describe the similarities and differences between impression management and people pleasing?

- Would you say impression management and people pleasing are two names for the same thing? Why or why not?

Pleasing Problems

5. Loving and serving others as an expression of our love for God is a biblical value. But at its core, people pleasing isn't about love of God or others. Several Scriptures offer insights about what distinguishes people pleasing from authentic love and service. Go around the group and have a different person read each passage aloud. As the verses are read, underline any words or phrases that stand out to you. You may wish to read through the list twice to give everyone time to listen and respond.

> Yet at the same time many even among the leaders believed in [Jesus]. But because of the Pharisees they would not openly acknowledge their faith for fear they would be put out of the synagogue; for they loved human praise more than praise from God (John 12:42–43).

> When we want human approval and esteem, and do what we do for the sake of it, God courteously stands aside because, by our wish, it does not concern him.
>
> **Dallas Willard,**
> **The Divine Conspiracy**

> Obviously, I'm not trying to win the approval of people, but of God. If pleasing people were my goal, I would not be Christ's servant (Galatians 1:10 NLT).   *(cont.)*

Our purpose is to please God, not people. He alone examines the motives of our hearts. Never once did we try to win you with flattery, as you well know. And God is our witness that we were not pretending to be your friends just to get your money! As for human praise, we have never sought it from you or anyone else (1 Thessalonians 2:4 – 6 NLT).

What insights do these passages provide about what distinguishes people pleasing from authentically loving God and others?

6. The John 12 passage notes how fear of losing social status (being put out of the synagogue) led some to compromise their faith in Christ. You could say they were afraid to be weird!

   • What examples come to mind of modern-day equivalents — ways in which people today might compromise their faith to avoid disapproval or loss of social status?

   • Ironically, the approval and social status those referenced in the passage were afraid of losing was in a religious setting, a synagogue. In what ways, if any, might this dynamic be present in your own faith community? In other words, how might seeking recognition or approval from other Christians actually prevent you from pleasing God?

7. The 1 Thessalonians passage implies that seeking to please people can be a way to manipulate and deceive them for personal gain. For example: feigning friendship to get someone's money.

   • In the John 12 passage, would you say that those who would not openly acknowledge their faith in Christ manipulated and deceived others for personal gain? Why or why not?

   • In your own efforts to gain approval or praise from others, what personal gain have you typically hoped to achieve? For example, more respect or esteem, sympathy, affection? In what subtle or overt ways have you manipulated or deceived in order to get it?

Fearing God

8. Many people-pleasing behaviors are motivated by fear — fear of not fitting in, not getting what we need, not being cared for or loved. But the Bible offers a different perspective on catering to other people's opinions.

> Fearing people is a dangerous trap, but trusting the LORD means safety (Proverbs 29:25 NLT).

> "Listen to me, you who know right from wrong, you who cherish my law in your hearts. Do not be afraid of people's scorn, nor fear their insults. For the moth will devour them as it devours clothing. The worm will eat at them as it eats wool. But my righteousness will last forever. My salvation will continue from generation to generation" (Isaiah 51:7 – 8 NLT).

- Looking back on your past experiences of impression management or people pleasing, how would you describe the "dangerous trap" you faced in those situations?

- The Isaiah passage contrasts the brevity of human opinion with the eternity of God's righteousness. Do you think this perspective will help you to resist people pleasing? Or is this one of those truths that looks good on Bible paper but is hard for you to realize in everyday life? Describe the reasons for your response.

- If you could fully embrace and live out the truth of the Isaiah passage, what changes would you hope to experience in your heart as well as in your relationships with God and others?

9. On the video, Craig says, "The fear of God is the best antidote for the fear of people.... When your God becomes bigger, the opinions of other people become smaller and you become weirder." One Scripture puts it this way:

> Serve only the LORD your God and fear him alone. Obey his commands, listen to his voice, and cling to him (Deuteronomy 13:4 NLT).

- The verse describes three ways we can serve and fear (revere, worship) God alone: (1) obey his commands, (2) listen to his voice, and (3) cling to him. Think of someone whose approval is important to you, perhaps too important. How might following these three commands make God bigger — and this person's opinion smaller — in your life?

- Of the three commands, which do you think will help you most when you are tempted to engage in impression management or people pleasing? Why?

Individual Activity: What I Want to Remember (2 Minutes)

Complete this activity on your own.

1. Briefly review the video outline and any notes you took.

2. In the space below, write down the most significant thing you gained in this session — from the teaching, activities, or discussions.

What I want to remember from this session ...

Closing Prayer

Close your time together with prayer.

Between-Sessions Personal Study

● READ AND REFLECT

Read chapters 7, 8, and 9 of *Weird*. Use the space below to note any insights or questions you want to bring to the next group session.

● GOD-PLEASING WEIRD

The Bible teaches that we are to love God and love others (Matthew 22:37 – 39). If, instead, anyone tried to convince us that we are to worship God and worship others, we'd never fall for it. We know that's not right. But we do fall for it. It happens every time we get caught in the trap of people-pleasing. Which is why people pleasing is more of a spiritual problem than a relational problem — it's misapplied worship.

People pleasing is worshiping the opinions of others rather than serving the opinion of God.   *Weird* video

1. For each of the statements below, rate the degree to which it describes you, using the following scale:

3 = Often true of me
2 = Frequently true of me
1 = Occasionally true of me
0 = Rarely true of me

a. _____ I want to be liked by everyone.

b. _____ I withhold my opinion to avoid potential conflict or disapproval.

c. _____ People say I am always smiling.

d. _____ I engage in impression management by subtly trying to make myself or my behavior look better.

e. _____ I can never do enough to please people.

f. _____ People consider me a great team player — cooperative, supportive, and always willing to pitch in.

g. _____ I tend to go along with what other people say or do.

h. _____ The harder I work, the more people will appreciate me.

i. _____ People will only like me if I am nice, pleasant, and friendly to them.

j. _____ Before making a decision, I am careful to consider whether or not it might upset anyone.

k. _____ I feel responsible for other people's happiness.

l. _____ People often describe me as warm, caring, happy, or full of fun.

m. _____ I feel guilty for not accomplishing enough or being enough to please others.

n. _____ I have very high standards for myself and can feel like a failure if I don't meet them.

o. _____ If I am not successful, I will be ignored, disrespected, or unloved.

p. _____ People have described me as a pushover, a martyr, or a doormat.

q. _____ Being rejected is one of the worst things that could happen to me.

r. _____ It's not who I am but what I do that counts.

s. _____ I am devastated if someone doesn't like me.

t. _____ It's very hard for me to deal with criticism.

Now transfer your responses to the grid and then add them together for a total.

QUESTION	MY RESPONSE (3,2,1,0)
a	
b	
c	
d	
e	
f	
g	
h	
i	
j	
k	
l	
m	
n	
o	
p	
q	
r	
s	
t	
TOTAL	

Next, write your total in the blank below and divide that number by 20 to determine your average response.

Example

$$\underline{35} \div \quad 20 \quad = \quad \underline{1.75}$$

Total   Average

$$\underline{} \div \quad 20 \quad = \quad \underline{}$$

Total   Average

If your average is ...	It's likely you are ...
2.5–3	Often a people pleaser
1.5–2.5	Frequently a people pleaser
.5–1.5	Occasionally a people pleaser
Less than .5	Rarely a people pleaser

Would you say your average response number seems true of you? Why or why not?

We have to be weird enough not to care what people think of who we are and how we live. Living for others' opinions is putting people ahead of God.

Weird, page 137

2. People pleasing is more than a personal issue; it's a spiritual issue. Consider the command below from Deuteronomy and an adapted version that imagines the same command from a people-pleasing perspective.

> Serve only the LORD your God and fear him alone. Obey his commands, listen to his voice, and cling to him (Deuteronomy 13:4 NLT).

> Serve only the people whose approval matters to you; fear their opinions alone. Obey their commands, listen to their voices, and cling to them. (People-Pleasing Adaptation)

What's your initial response to the people-pleasing adaptation?

3. Though brief, Deuteronomy 13:4 packs in five commands. Listed in the the chart on page 63 are the five commands. For each command, consider (1) what you imagine the people-pleasing version of this command might be, and (2) why someone might want to follow this command. Note your responses in the second column. See example below.

Example

GOD'S COMMANDS	PEOPLE-PLEASERS' COMMANDS
Serve only the Lord your God.	Serve only other people, especially people whose opinions matter most.
	Why? Because then people will like me and that helps me to feel needed, accepted, and important.

GOD'S COMMANDS	PEOPLE-PLEASERS' COMMANDS
Serve only the Lord your God.	
	Why?
Fear him alone.	
	Why?
Obey his commands.	
	Why?
Listen to his voice.	
	Why?
Cling to him.	
	Why?

- Briefly review your chart on page 63. What common phrases or themes do you notice in your responses to the "Why?" questions?

- Again referring to your chart, place a checkmark next to the "Why?" response that resonates most with you. In what way, if any, might your response reflect something you are missing in your relationship with God?

> Becoming obsessed with what people think about you is the quickest way to forget what God thinks about you.
>
> *Weird* video

4. The Bible includes many statements that reveal what God thinks about us. After reading each of the verses on page 65, respond with an "I" statement that summarizes the truth that verse reveals about how God sees you.

Example

Put on your new nature, created to be like God — truly righteous and holy (Ephesians 4:24 NLT).

I have a new nature.
I am created to be like God — righteous and holy.

But to all who believed him and accepted him, he gave the right to become children of God (John 1:12 NLT).

I am a child of God.

Honor God by accepting each other, as Christ has accepted you (Romans 15:7 CEV).

Even before he made the world, God loved us and chose us in Christ to be holy and without fault in his eyes (Ephesians 1:4 NLT).

Yet God, with undeserved kindness, declares that we are righteous. He did this through Christ Jesus when he freed us from the penalty for our sins (Romans 3:24 NLT).

But now in Christ Jesus you who once were far away have been brought near by the blood of Christ (Ephesians 2:13).

The fear of God is the best antidote for the fear of people.
Weird video

5. To fear God is to have a reverent awe of God. It's a holy sense of "divine wow" that puts everything else in perspective. Consider some of the Bible's wisdom about fearing God and living to please him.

And now, Israel, what does the LORD your God require of you? He requires only that you fear the LORD your God, and live in a way that pleases him, and love him and serve him with all your heart and soul (Deuteronomy 10:12 NLT). *(cont.)*

The Kingdom of God is . . . living a life of goodness and peace and joy in the Holy Spirit. If you serve Christ with this attitude, you will please God, and others will approve of you, too (Romans 14:17 – 19 NLT).

For God is working in you, giving you the desire and the power to do what pleases him (Philippians 2:13 NLT).

- "Fear the LORD your God" is the first requirement listed in the Deuteronomy passage. Why do you think it's first? How might fear or a reverent awe of God support the remaining requirements in that verse?

- What insight or encouragement do these passages provide about pleasing God in your own life?

Fear. That's not normally a word we like to hear. But attach fear to God and it's a beautiful thing. It puts other people in perspective; their opinions get smaller. It puts you in perspective; you can't please everyone, but you can please God. And it puts God in perspective; holy, all-knowing, all-powerful, ever-present Alpha and Omega of the universe and beyond, thank you very much. That's holy fear in all its weird and wonderful glory.

WEIRD MAKES YOU TRULY SEXY

This side of the fall, we often understand our sexuality through a glass darkly. Our task as Christians is to pick our way through sexuality's distortions and into sexuality's wholeness.

RICHARD J. FOSTER, *THE CHALLENGE OF THE DISCIPLINED LIFE*

Group Discussion: Checking In (5 Minutes)

Welcome to session 5 of *Weird*. A key part of getting to know God better is sharing your journey with others. Before watching the video, briefly check in with each other about your experiences since the last session. For example:

- What insights did you discover in the personal study or in the chapters you read from the *Weird* book?
- How did the last session impact your daily life or your relationship with God?
- What questions would you like to ask the other members of your group?

Video: Weird Makes You Truly Sexy (17 Minutes)

Play the video segment for session 5. As you watch, use the outline (pages 68–70) to follow along or to take notes on anything that stands out to you.

Notes

What's normal today ...

- premarital sex
- pornography
- lust
- affairs
- divorce
- guilt, regret, fears
- diseases

Up to 65 percent of husbands and 55 percent of wives commit adultery before the age of forty.

A definition of weird: putting distance between you and temptation.

"Flee from sexual immorality. All other sins a man commits are outside his body, but he who sins sexually sins against his own body" (1 Corinthians 6:18).

The Greek word for "flee" is *pheugō* (fyoo´-go). It means to run away, shun, escape, distance oneself.

Normal is ...

- How far can I go?
- How much can I get away with?
- How much can I enjoy without getting caught?

Weird is ...

How far can I stay away from that which could hurt me in the worst sort of way?

"But among you there must not be even a hint of sexual immorality, or of any kind of impurity, or of greed, because these are improper for God's holy people" (Ephesians 5:3).

Weird places to draw the line:

1. Dress for spiritual success. If you've got it, you don't have to show it.
2. No sleepovers or playing house.
3. Avoid dangerous places, whatever that is to you. Keep a wise distance between you and temptation.
4. Guard your eyes, your mind, and your heart against whatever makes you vulnerable.

"For once you were full of darkness, but now you have light from the Lord. So live as people of light!" (Ephesians 5:8 NLT)

Group Discussion: Weird Makes You Truly Sexy (36 Minutes)

Take a few minutes to talk about what you just watched.

1. What part of the teaching had the most impact on you?

2. In Christian circles, which is more uncomfortable for you to talk about: money or sex? Why?

> Why should we be ashamed to discuss what God was not ashamed to create?
>
> Howard Hendricks, Husbands and Wives

Normal and Sex

3. Briefly review the following list of selected Christian books on love, dating, and sexuality. Which title or titles best express where you are right now when it comes to sex? Describe the reasons for your response.

☐ Nobody Told Me
☐ The Purity Code
☐ Pure Excitement
☐ Temptation
☐ Lady in Waiting
☐ Common Mistakes Singles Make
☐ When Dreams Come True
☐ Sex Detox
☐ Datable

☐ Breaking Free
☐ In the Mood Again
☐ Turn Up the Heat
☐ Escape from Intimacy
☐ Sex 101
☐ Not Ready for Marriage, Not Ready for Sex
☐ No Time for Sex
☐ Love, Sex, and Happily Ever After

☐ A Celebration of Sex after 50

☐ Battered Love

☐ Crazy Good Sex

☐ What's Love Got to Do with It?

☐ Sex Has a Price Tag

☐ I Kissed Dating Goodbye

☐ Quest for Love

☐ Is That All He Thinks About?

☐ Married but Not Engaged

☐ Shattered Vows

☐ How Far Can You Go?

☐ Reclaiming Intimacy

☐ Seductive Delusions

4. On the video, Craig describes what constitutes normal today when it comes to sex: premarital sex, lust, affairs, etc. Some studies have found that the incidence of these behaviors is the same among Christians as it is among non-Christians. In other words, Christians get divorced, have affairs, and consume pornography at the same levels non-Christians do.

• What unique challenges do you think Christians might face in dealing with these issues?

• How does your Christian community help or fail to help you with your attitudes, behaviors, or other concerns related to sex?

> Sex is power, real power. There is nothing neutral or passive about it. It is alive with spiritual energy seeking to make a bid for supremacy over the hearts of men and women.
>
> Richard Foster, *The Challenge of the Disciplined Life*

Weird and Sex

5. Craig offers this definition of weird: *keeping a great distance between you and temptation.* Here is how the apostle Paul says it:

> Run from sexual sin! No other sin so clearly affects the body as this one does. For sexual immorality is a sin against your own body. Don't you realize that your body is the temple of the Holy Spirit, who lives in you and

was given to you by God? You do not belong to yourself, for God bought you with a high price. So you must honor God with your body (1 Corinthians 6:18 – 20 NLT).

- Paul presents three truths about bodies: (1) sexual immorality is a sin against your own body, (2) your body is the temple of the Holy Spirit, and (3) you do not belong to yourself. When you consider what might be required of you in order to run from sexual sin, which of these truths is most compelling or helpful to you?

- The Greek word Paul uses for honor is *doxazō* (dox-ad´-zo), which means to praise or glorify. The root word *doxa* is the basis for the English word "doxology." Paul uses the word when he describes the "glory" (*doxa*) of Moses' face after being in God's presence (2 Corinthians 3:7). Moses literally reflected God's glory in ways people could see and recognize.[4] Do you think it's possible for Christians today to honor God with their bodies — to physically reflect God's glory — in ways people can see and recognize? Describe the reasons for your response.

6. The apostle Paul also cautions against ever considering ourselves beyond temptation:

> If you think you are standing strong, be careful not to fall. The temptations in your life are no different from what others experience. And God is faithful. He will not allow the temptation to be more than you can stand. When you are tempted, he will show you a way out so that you can endure (1 Corinthians 10:12 – 13 NLT).

For a fresh perspective on this familiar passage, read it again from *The Message*:

---

4. It is interesting to note that *doxa* is directly linked to the Old Testament concept of *kābôd* (ka-vode´) — God's glory — and especially how it is evidenced in visually observable ways. "When it is used of God, it does not mean God in his essential nature, but the luminous manifestation of his person, his glorious revelation of himself. Characteristically, *kābôd* is linked with verbs of seeing, and appearing." Sverre Aalen, "Glory, Honour," *New International Dictionary of New Testament Theology*, vol. 2, Colin Brown, gen. ed. (Grand Rapids: Zondervan, 1978, 1986), 45.

Don't be so naive and self-confident. You're not exempt. You could fall flat on your face as easily as anyone else. Forget about self-confidence; it's useless. Cultivate God-confidence. No test or temptation that comes your way is beyond the course of what others have had to face. All you need to remember is that God will never let you down; he'll never let you be pushed past your limit; he'll always be there to help you come through it (1 Corinthians 10:12 – 13 MSG).

- In what ways might thinking you are beyond sexual temptation make you more vulnerable to it?

- How would you describe the difference between self-confidence and God-confidence? If possible, briefly share examples of both kinds of confidence, either from your own life or from the life of someone you know.

- In general, do you feel that you are always aware of "a way out" when you are tempted? If so, what determines whether or not you take the way out? If not, what leads you to feel that you have no option except to give in when you are tempted?

Turn the Light On

7. Among the signs that something may be a temptation or a sin in our lives is a desire to hide or to keep it a secret. But the promise of Scripture is that our freedom and healing begin when we invite the light of Christ into our darkness.

For once you were full of darkness, but now you have light from the Lord. So live as people of light! For this light within you produces only what is good and right and true. Carefully determine what pleases the Lord. Take no part in the worthless deeds of evil and darkness; instead, expose them (Ephesians 5:8 – 11 NLT).

- Share an experience that could be described as "living in the light." For example, it might be when you initially came to know Christ, a time you resisted temptation, or an experience of following God's leading. What was the experience like? How did it impact your relationship with God?

- If you feel comfortable doing so, complete the following sentences:

  When it comes to sex, I know I'm living in darkness when ...

  When it comes to sex, I know I'm living in the light when ...

8. According to the Ephesians passage, the light of Christ within you "produces only what is good and right and true."

  - What would you characterize as good and right and true about your sex life right now?

  - What hopes do you have for this area of your life?

> The full truth about sex is this: It is both sacred and polluted, holy and desecrated. The sacredness of sex is not based on how we treat it or mistreat it. Its sacredness is based on its essence, which comes from God. Sex is holy because God created it to be holy.
>
> Tim Alan Gardner,
> *Sacred Sex*

Individual Activity: What I Want to Remember (2 Minutes)

Complete this activity on your own.

1. Briefly review the video outline and any notes you took.

2. In the space below, write down the most significant thing you gained in this session — from the teaching, activities, or discussions.

   What I want to remember from this session ...

Closing Prayer

Close your time together with prayer.

Between-Sessions Personal Study

● READ AND REFLECT

Read chapters 10, 11, and 12 of *Weird*. Use the space below to note any insights or questions you want to bring to the next group session.

● WHOLE, CHASTE SEX

"All believers," writes Richard Foster, "whether male or female, whether single, married, divorced, widowed or remarried — are called to fidelity in their sexual relationships." [5] Fidelity is faithfulness — to a spouse, to ourselves, to God. To be faithful is to be loyal, truthful, and steady in our loving commitments. In fidelity, we honor our God-given sexuality by celebrating its goodness and protecting its vulnerabilities. And, in deep trust, we surrender its hurts and brokenness to the God who forgives, heals, and makes all things new.

> The collateral damage of sexual impurity is painful, emotional, and deeply spiritual. . . . In the culture we live in today, virtually no one walks around without some sexual wounds. Your mind is injured, your soul is numb. While you can protect your injury and prevent it from getting worse, remember that only God can heal it. And he wants to.
>
> *Weird*, pages 165, 173

1. Collateral damage is damage that is unanticipated or unintentional. We didn't mean for it to happen or want it to happen, but it did. Use the following prompts to briefly identify some of the collateral damage or injuries from your own sexual history.

   Injuries to my mind and thoughts . . .

---

5. Richard J. Foster, *The Challenge of the Disciplined Life* (San Francisco: Harper & Row, 1985), 150.

Injuries to my body ...

Injuries to my soul and my relationship with God ...

Injuries to my relationships ...

Other injuries or damage ...

2. What impact have these experiences had on how you view or experience sex and intimacy?

3. One way to think about what it means to be sexually healthy, whole, and holy is the concept of chastity. To be chaste can mean merely to abstain from sex, but it also has a larger meaning. In his book *Holy Longing*, author Ronald Rolheiser describes it this way:

> For a Christian, sex always needs the protection of a healthy chastity.... Chastity is not the same thing as celibacy.... Chastity has to do with all experiencing. It is about the appropriateness of any experience. Ultimately, chastity is reverence — and sin, all sin, is irreverence. To be chaste is to experience people, things, places, entertainment, the phases of our lives, and sex in a way that does not violate them or ourselves. To be chaste is to experience things reverently.[6]

---

6. Ronald Rolheiser, *The Holy Longing* (New York: Doubleday, 1999), 201 – 202.

In *Real Sex*, author Lauren Winner echoes this theme:

> To practice sexual chastity is not to guarantee our own personal purity or righteousness. It is rather to strive to do sex, to have relationships with other people, and to comport our bodies and our desires in ways that perfectly love God and worthily magnify his name.[7]

- In what ways would you say your sex life now is reverent and/or irreverent?

- Think about the things your body does in the course of a typical day — morning, afternoon, evening. What thoughts come to mind when you consider what it would mean to "comport your body and your desires in ways that perfectly love God"?

  In the morning …

  In the afternoon …

  In the evening …

4. Although the apostle Paul doesn't use the word "chastity," he strongly affirms the importance of putting our bodies in reverent service to God:

> Do not let any part of your body become an instrument of evil to serve sin. Instead, give yourselves completely to God, for you were dead, but now you have new life. So use your whole body as an instrument to do what is right for the glory of God (Romans 6:13 NLT).

---

7. Lauren Winner, *Real Sex* (Grand Rapids: Brazos Press, 2005), 156.

It is sometimes tempting to compartmentalize sexual thinking and behaviors — to put them in a separate category from the values and beliefs we practice in other areas of our lives. Paul counters this way of thinking and stresses the importance of giving our bodies — our whole selves — completely to God.

- In what ways, if any, do you compartmentalize your sexual thinking and behaviors?

- What appeals to you about the idea of wholeness, of not being compartmentalized in your sexual thinking and behaviors?

What God makes new is often so much better than anything you ever imagined before. No matter what sin you find yourself in, turn to God. Let him forgive, heal, and restore.
Weird, pages 157 – 158

5. Forgiveness is for the wrongs we have done — to God, to others, to ourselves. Healing is for the injuries we have suffered, either through our own decisions or through no fault of our own. Restoration is for the broken soul; it puts us back together, whole in the sight of God.

Write a brief prayer to God, inviting him into your sexuality. Tell him about any wrongs, injuries, or brokenness you have in the area of sex and intimacy. Ask him for what you need from him.

In *The Challenge of the Disciplined Life*, Richard Foster writes:

Our sexuality is intimately tied to who we are as spiritual persons. The spiritual life enhances our sexuality and gives it direction. Our sexuality gives an earthy wholeness to our spirituality. Our spirituality and our sexuality come into a working harmony in the life of the kingdom of God.[8]

We are called to fidelity in our sexual relationships, to bring body and soul together in working harmony. To be whole and holy, flesh and blood, intimate and chaste — utterly surrendered to Christ, the lover of our souls.

8. Foster, *The Challenge of the Disciplined Life*, 100.

THE WEIRDEST BLESSING POSSIBLE

God loves it when his people love what he loves and hate what he hates. He loves it when his followers are disheartened by the things that dishearten him and emboldened by the things he's passionate about. This is the backbone of understanding holy discontent — a simple alliance between God and normal, everyday, earthbound human beings who happen to find themselves stirred up by the exact same thing that stirs the heart of the Creator.

BILL HYBELS, *LIVING AND LEADING FROM YOUR HOLY DISCONTENT*

Group Discussion: Checking In (5 Minutes)

Welcome to session 6 of *Weird*. A key part of getting to know God better is sharing your journey with others. Before watching the video, briefly check in with each other about your experiences since the last session. For example:

- What insights did you discover in the personal study or in the chapters you read from the *Weird* book?
- How did the last session impact your daily life or your relationship with God?
- What questions would you like to ask the other members of your group?

Video: The Weirdest Blessing Possible (17 Minutes)

Play the video segment for session 6. As you watch, use the outline (pages 82–84) to follow along or to take notes on anything that stands out to you.

Notes

It's normal to want to avoid the things that bother you or disturb you.

Weird people stop and embrace the pain of what bothers them.

God wants to bless you with a burden.

Holy discontent: something in your soul that bothers you so much you say, "I'm not okay with this."

Weird questions to uncover your burden:

1. What is it that breaks your heart? *Example: Nehemiah (Nehemiah 1:3 – 4)*

2. What is it that makes you righteously angry? *Example: Moses (Exodus 2:11 – 12)*

3. What is it you care about that other people don't seem to care about? *Example: David (1 Samuel 17:26)*

Finish this sentence: I'm burdened by _____

_____.

Two things to do once you identify your burden:

1. Let your burden ruin you. Let it mess you up.

   " 'Woe to me,' I cried, 'I am ruined.' For I am a man of unclean lips, and I live among a people of unclean lips, and my eyes have seen the King, the LORD Almighty" (Isaiah 6:5).

2. Let your burden move you to action.

You are holy. The Greek word for "holy" is *hagios* (hag´-ee-os). It means to be set apart, to be different. You are no longer normal.

"Then I heard the voice of the LORD saying, 'Whom shall I send? And who will go for us?' And I said, 'Here am I. Send me!' " (Isaiah 6:8)

Be weird enough, bold enough, and different enough to say to God, "Yes; wherever you want me to go, here I am, Lord; send me."

Group Discussion: The Weirdest Blessing Possible (36 Minutes)

Take a few minutes to talk about what you just watched.

1. What part of the teaching had the most impact on you?

2. How do you respond to the idea that God wants to bless you with a burden?

Normal Pain Avoidance

3. In the course of a regular week, what kind of information do you routinely avoid because it's too uncomfortable, too painful, or provides too much reality about suffering? For example: leaflets about missing children, articles about violence against women, news coverage of military conflicts, billboards about cruelty to animals, appeals on behalf of those living in extreme poverty.

4. What thoughts go through your head when you choose to avoid exposing yourself to such information? For example: *I don't want to know that. That's too overwhelming. I can't do anything about it, so why torture myself?*

5. How do you imagine it might impact you if you were to more routinely engage this kind of information rather than avoid it?

Weird Pain Pursuit

6. The Scripture passages listed below describe various responses to suffering. Go around the group and have a different person read each passage aloud. As the verses are read the first time, consider what you hear from the perspective of a person who is suffering. On the second reading, consider what you hear from the perspective of an observer, a witness to someone else's suffering. Underline any words or phrases that stand out to you. You may wish to read through the list multiple times to give everyone time to listen, consider the texts from both perspectives, and respond.

> My relatives stay far away, and my friends have turned against me. My family is gone, and my close friends have forgotten me (Job 19:13 – 14 NLT).

> He was despised and rejected — a man of sorrows, acquainted with deepest grief. We turned our backs on him and looked the other way. He was despised, and we did not care (Isaiah 53:3 NLT).

> I hurt with the hurt of my people. I mourn and am overcome with grief. Is there no medicine in Gilead? Is there no physician there? Why is there no healing for the wounds of my people? (Jeremiah 8:21 – 22 NLT)

> The place God calls you to is the place where your deep gladness and the world's deep hunger meet.
>
> Frederick Buechner,
> *Wishful Thinking*

> Jesus saw the huge crowd as he stepped from the boat, and he had compassion on them because they were like sheep without a shepherd (Mark 6:34 NLT).

• What are your observations when you think about these passages from both perspectives — that of someone who suffers and that of someone who observes suffering?

• In what ways do you relate, or struggle to relate, to each perspective?

7. Craig teaches that weird people embrace the pain of what bothers them. They ask God to bless them with a divine burden, a "holy discontent" about something that's not right in the world. Accepting this burden is part of what it means to partner with God in his redeeming work (Ephesians 2:10; 1 Corinthians 1:9).

Two passages below describe the work God does to put things right in the world. As you read the passages aloud, imagine that what you are hearing is a description of God's response to his own divine burden.

He gives justice to the oppressed and food to the hungry. The LORD frees the prisoners. The LORD opens the eyes of the blind. The LORD lifts up those who are weighed down. The LORD loves the godly. The LORD protects the foreigners among us. He cares for the orphans and widows, but he frustrates the plans of the wicked (Psalm 146:7 – 9 NLT).

"The Spirit of the Lord is on me, because he has anointed me to proclaim good news to the poor. He has sent me to proclaim freedom for the prisoners and recovery of sight for the blind, to set the oppressed free, to proclaim the year of the Lord's favor" (Luke 4:18 – 19).

- How would you describe the pain God must embrace in order to do the things the passages describe? For example, what is the pain of someone who suffers injustice, who is poor, or who feels forgotten (rather than favored) by the Lord?

- Do you think it's possible to have a divine burden without engaging pain or experiencing some kind of discomfort? Describe the reasons for your response.

- How do these passages inform your understanding of what it might mean for you to experience your own burden from God?

A Divine Burden

8. Discovering your divine burden might happen quickly or it may take additional study and prayerful discernment over a period of time. On the video, Craig offers three questions to help you begin to explore what your burden might be: (1) What is it that breaks your heart? (2) What is it that makes you righteously angry? (3) What is it you care about that other people don't seem to care about?

   Choose the question that sparks the most energy or interest in you. Then, using the number below that corresponds to the question you chose, complete all three sentences with the first thing that comes to mind. Resist the temptation to overthink your response! Go with your initial instinct.

   (1) What breaks my heart in the world is ...

   What breaks my heart in my community is ...

   What breaks my heart among people I know is ...

   (2) What makes me angry in the world is ...

   What makes me angry in my community is ...

   What makes me angry among people I know is ...

(3) What I care about that other people don't seem to care about in the world is …

What I care about that other people don't seem to care about in my community is …

What I care about that other people don't seem to care about among the people I know is …

9. The hoped-for impact of responding to a divine burden is often clear — the poor receive resources, the illiterate learn to read, the grieving are comforted, lives are changed. But those who bear the burdens and reach out to help others are also impacted. What hopes do you have about how living out your divine burden might impact you? For example, how might it impact your relationship with God, the kind of person you want to become, your outlook on life, or how you relate to others?

Individual Activity: What I Want to Remember (2 Minutes)

Complete this activity on your own.

1. Briefly review the video outline and any notes you took.

2. In the space below, write down the most significant thing you gained in this session — from the teaching, activities, or discussions.

   What I want to remember from this session . . .

Closing Prayer

Close your time together with prayer.

As an option, use the Franciscan Benediction (page 90) to mark the end of this study and to close your gathering.

1. Appoint one person to read the benediction aloud.

2. Set aside your study materials so your hands and lap are empty and then settle into a comfortable position. As you begin, you may wish to close your eyes, inhale deeply, and exhale slowly. Silently ask God to use this blessing to speak to you.

3. The reader prayerfully reads each line aloud, allowing 1 to 2 minutes of silence after each one, and concludes the prayer time with "Amen."

A Franciscan Benediction

May God bless you with discomfort at easy answers, half-truths, and superficial relationships, so that you may live deep within your heart.

(*Pause, 1 – 2 minutes.*)

May God bless you with anger at injustice, oppression, and exploitation of people, so that you may work for justice, freedom, and peace.

(*Pause, 1 – 2 minutes.*)

May God bless you with tears to shed for those who suffer from pain, rejection, and starvation, so that you may reach out your hand to comfort them and to turn their pain into joy.

(*Pause, 1 – 2 minutes.*)

And may God bless you with enough foolishness to believe that you can make a difference in this world, so that you can do what others claim cannot be done.

(*Pause, 1 – 2 minutes.*)

May God bless you with the weirdest blessing possible — his divine burden.

Amen.

Final Personal Study

● READ AND REFLECT

Read chapters 13, 14, 15, and the conclusion of *Weird*. Use the space below to note any insights or questions.

● PURSUING BURDENS

God wants to give you a weird blessing: a divine burden to make a difference. This kind of blessing is rich in purpose and full of holy adventure, but it is also anchored to the harsh realities of a broken world. As you open yourself to the blessing, you open yourself to the pain as well. It's the weird way things work for anyone who wants to follow Jesus — a Savior who took on all the sin and hurt we could not bear in order to bless us with a life we couldn't have any other way.

> Most of us feel good when we avoid burdens — after all, isn't life hard enough? Why ask God for more trials, trauma, and tears? It's normal to want to avoid pain — human even. But God didn't put us here on earth just to feel good and enjoy ourselves. He doesn't give us our lives so we can master techniques in avoiding pain.
>
> He puts us here to make an eternal difference.
>
> He puts us here to show everyone around us how much he loves them.
>
> He puts us here to be his hands and feet, his body and his heart.
>
> *Weird*, page 207

1. We associate a burden with an unwelcome event, an unavoidable misfortune. But not all burdens are bad or even uninvited — the burden of bearing and raising children, for example. Parents willingly endure many hardships — physical, emotional, financial, spiritual — and most wouldn't have it any other way. The blessing of children makes the burden of having them more than worth bearing. What burdens have you willingly taken on because you believed the blessing or reward would be worth it?

   How does your experience of these burdens with blessings inform your understanding of what it might mean to invite God to give you a divine burden?

2. The burden-blessing theme is evident in many passages throughout the Bible. Read and reflect on what each of the following passages teaches about burdens and blessings.

   > For God called you to do good, even if it means suffering, just as Christ suffered for you. He is your example, and you must follow in his steps (1 Peter 2:21 NLT).

   > So if you are suffering in a manner that pleases God, keep on doing what is right, and trust your lives to the God who created you, for he will never fail you (1 Peter 4:19 NLT).

   How these passages help me understand burdens and blessings ...

   > Those who live only to satisfy their own sinful nature will harvest decay and death from that sinful nature. But those who live to please the Spirit will harvest everlasting life from the Spirit. So let's not get tired of doing what is good. At just the right time we will reap a harvest of blessing if we don't give up. Therefore, whenever we have the opportunity, we should do good to everyone — especially to those in the family of faith (Galatians 6:8 – 10 NLT).

   How this passage helps me understand burdens and blessings ...

Our people must learn to do good by meeting the urgent needs of others; then they will not be unproductive (Titus 3:14 NLT).

For a fresh perspective on this verse, read it again from *The Message*:

Our people have to learn to be diligent in their work so that all necessities are met (especially among the needy) and they don't end up with nothing to show for their lives (Titus 3:14 MSG).

How this passage helps me understand burdens and blessings ...

God put you on earth with a divine assignment—something prepared in advance for you to do. ... The things that make us sad, the things that make us righteously angry, or the things we care about that others don't are often a key that unlocks our reason for living. It's our burden.

Weird, page 214

3. Whether you have a good idea of what your divine assignment is or you're just beginning to investigate, you can trust that God is out ahead of you. He has already planted the seeds of a divine burden in your life — in your personality, your gifts, and your experiences. Sometimes those seeds are hidden in formative events — experiences or relationships that got our attention or marked us in some way. Here are some examples:

Church was lifeless. When I was in high school, I was embarrassed to invite my friends.

My parents couldn't afford health insurance. They lost everything when my dad got pancreatic cancer.

My mom wasn't married when she got pregnant. I grew up feeling like I was unwanted.

I read a news story about the widespread use of rape as a tool of war in the Congo.

There was a baby in the apartment next to ours who cried all the time. I don't think her parents ever held her.

When I was a kid, we had a neighbor who used to beat his dog.

My sister is an addict.

Use the prompts below to briefly identify some of your formative events — experiences or relationships that marked you in some way.

- Things I experienced in childhood ...

- Things I've read or seen (in books, online, on television, in movies) ...

- Things I've witnessed that moved me emotionally or made me cry ...

- Things I've seen while traveling abroad (or heard from others who have traveled) ...

- Things I've experienced in church ...

- Things I've experienced in difficult relationships ...

- Other formative experiences ...

4. One of the key characteristics of a divine burden is that it ignites a fire in you. You experience something that just isn't right and your gut reaction is, *This shouldn't be. I can't stand this. This turns my stomach. God didn't intend this. Why doesn't somebody do something about this?* Use the three

questions Craig presented on the video to reflect on the kinds of things that ignite a fire in you.

- What is it that breaks your heart?

- What is it that makes you righteously angry?

- What is it you care about that other people don't seem to care about?

5. Briefly review your responses to questions 3 and 4.
   - What words or themes stand out most to you?

   - Describe those words or themes as a declaration of truth. For example: *Church should feel wildly alive and relevant. No child should feel unwanted. Sexual violence must end.*

   - Based on your declaration(s) of truth, what divine burden do you want to learn more about or think God might be calling you to?

> If you really want to discover and develop the burden that uniquely connects you to the heart of God, you have to have courage. You have to risk. You have to do something— anything—to alleviate the suffering you've identified and embraced as your own.
>
> *Weird*, page 211

6. Whether you are crystal clear about your calling or still have some prayerful discernment to do, there is always a next step to take. It might include focused prayer, additional study, conversations with someone who has expertise or wisdom, fundraising, volunteer work, blogging, pulling a team together, or anything else that gets you closer to your divine calling. You can't do everything, but you can do something.

• A next step I can take to learn more about this burden is ...

• A next step I can take to pursue this burden is ...

In her book *One Thousand Gifts*, author Ann Voskamp assures us that God is more than equal to the tasks he gives:

> There is always enough God. He has no end. He calls us to serve, and it is him whom we serve, but he, very God, kneels down to serve us as we serve. The servant-hearted never serve alone. Spend the whole of your one wild and beautiful life investing in many lives and God simply will not be outdone.[9]

God put you on earth with a divine assignment — a weird blessing with your name on it. Will you take a risk and open your heart? Surrender your wild and beautiful life? Allow God to love the world through you? God stands by, eager to bless.

---

9. Ann Voskamp, *One Thousand Gifts* (Grand Rapids: Zondervan, 2011), 197.